If we have
no peace,
it is because we
have forgotten
that we belong
to each other.

Mother Teresa

ROSE

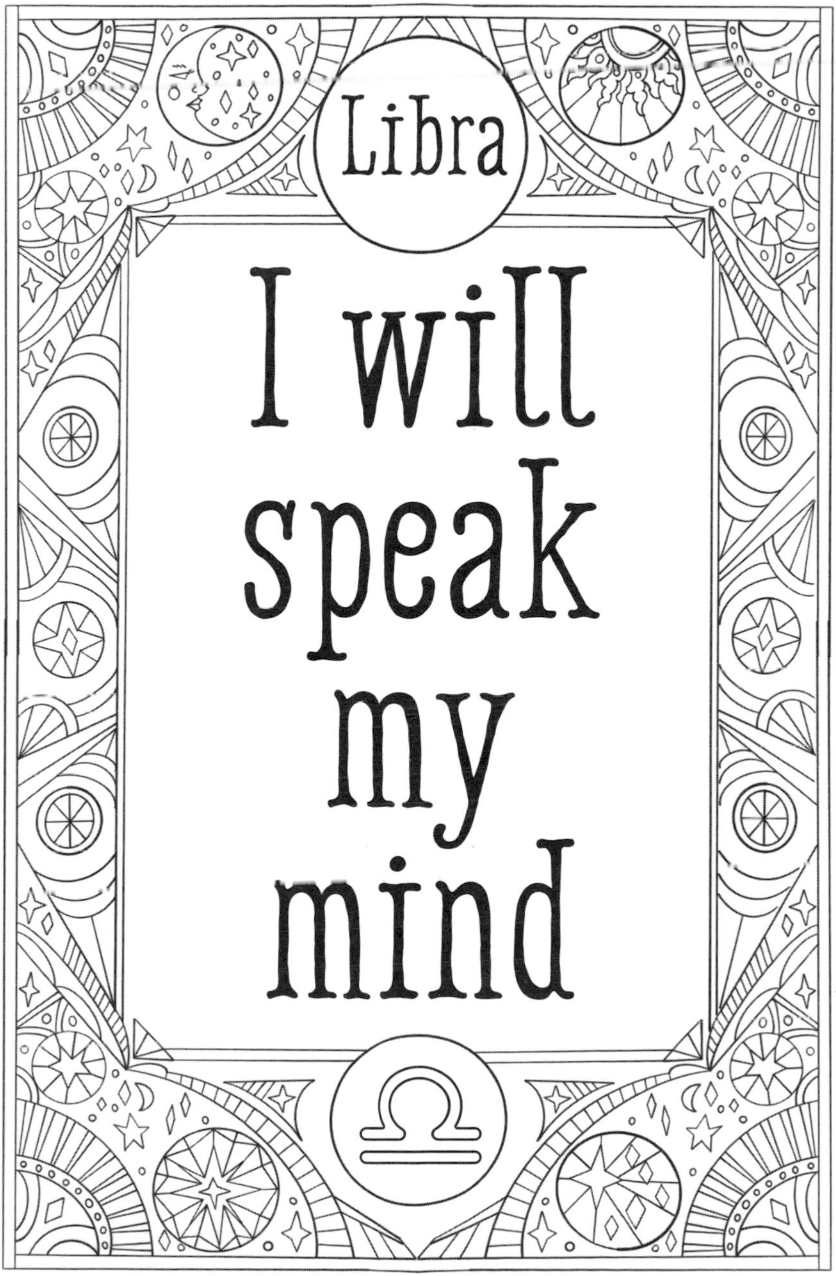
Libra
I will speak my mind

autumn

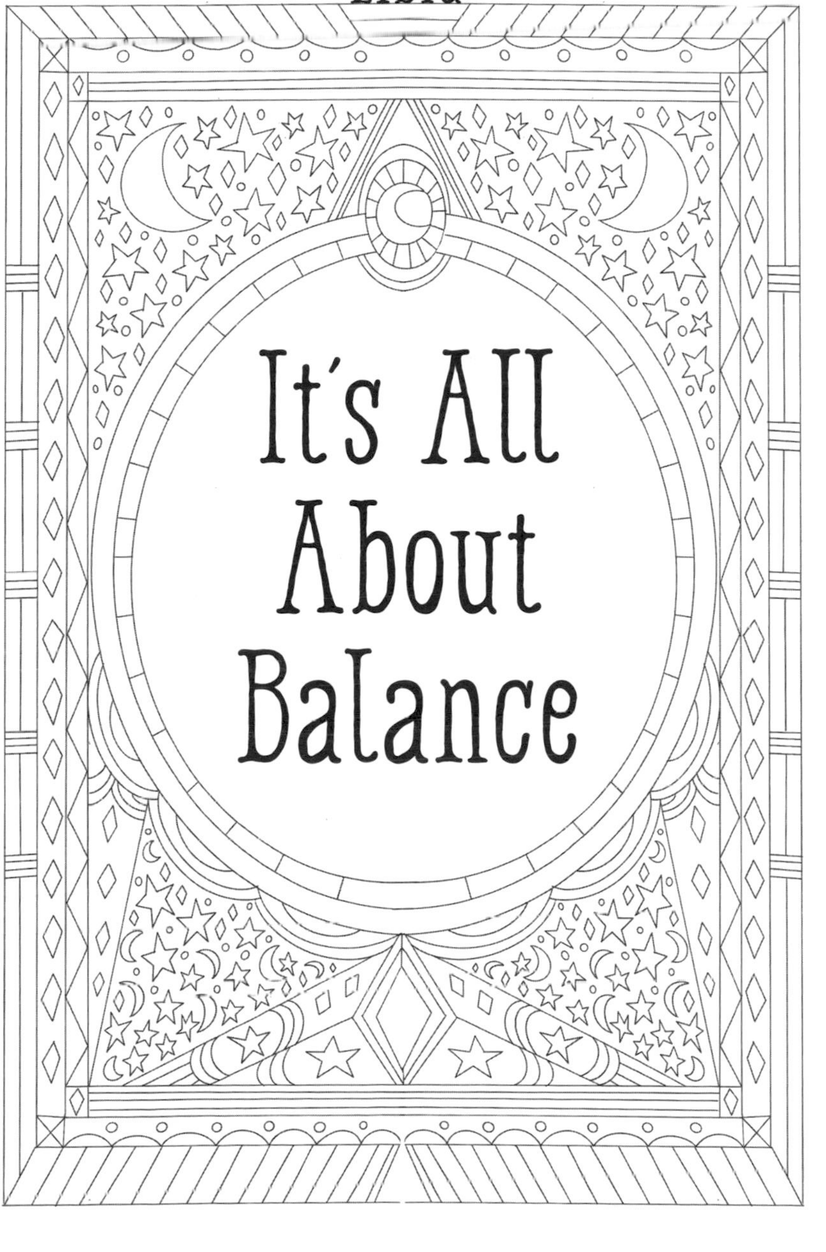
It's All
About
Balance

Libra
Ruled by Venus

libra

Creative

CHARMING

STYLISH

DIPLOMATIC

Witty

RULING HOUSE
7
The House of Partnerships

LIBRA

I am confident in being who I am

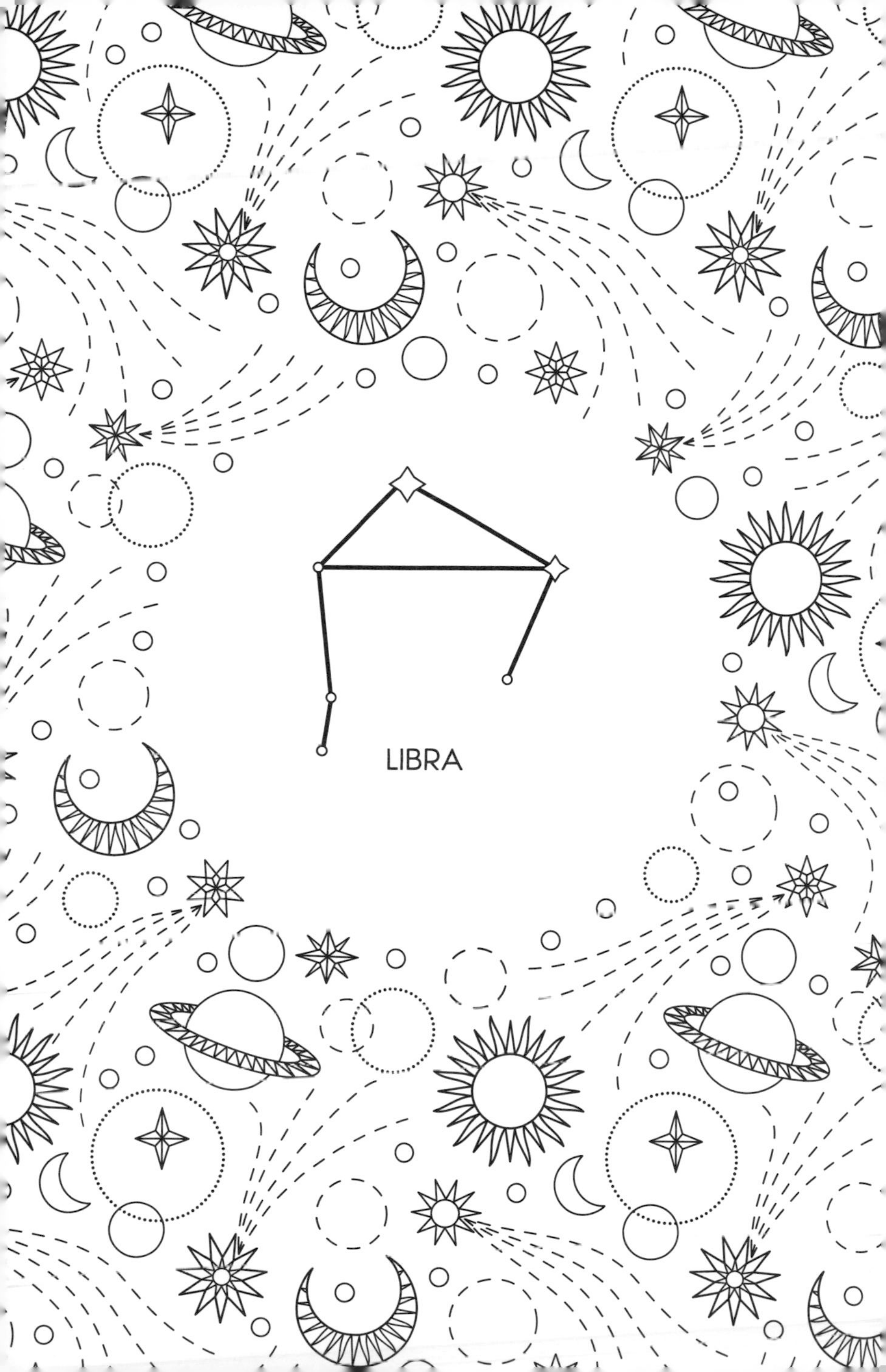
LIBRA

Aries
Taurus
Gemini
Cancer
Leo
Virgo
Libra
Scorpio
Sagittarius
Capricorn
Aquarius
Pisces

Air Signs
Aquarius
Libra
Gemini

LET THE STARS LEAD THE WAY

Image by Andrea Lauren © Simon & Schuster, Inc.

LIBRA

September 23–October 22